MW00914012

Sock Monkey Life

By

Kate Taylor

&

Jeffrey Underwood

Acknowledgments

To John Nelson who patented the red heeled socks

To Rockford, Illinois where the "Sock Monkey Madness Festival" is celebrated every year

To my family who has endured the embarrassment of my insanity when I bring my sock monkeys everywhere and make them stop for photographs

To Jeffrey Underwood, co-author and supplier of unlimited enthusiasm and support for my writing

To my sock monkeys, always loyal and open to adventures

Introduction

Sock monkeys first emerged in 1932. That was the year that the Nelson Knitting Company added the trademarked red heel to its socks. It was this distinctive red heel that provided the red mouth for sock monkeys.

Sock monkeys are popular even today. Many folks hunt for vintage sock monkeys or make their own. New sock monkeys may be striped or spotted, but there's nothing like the original.

Kate Taylor bought her first sock monkeys just a few years ago. They were vintage monkeys and had a quality about them, that she knew they had been hugged many times.

Kate learned about the 'birth' of sock monkeys. You will share in a birth in the pages to follow. Witness as Uno Bambino comes to life!

Most of the time, Henrx and Kashie, as she named the sock monkeys, lived on top of an old book case. One year, Kate had the opportunity to go on vacation. She decided to bring the sock monkeys with her and live vicariously through them for the week. They went everywhere with Kate and her family. Many times, passersby would stop to watch as Kate positioned the pair of monkeys to take photos of them. After a couple of days, locals and vacationers could be heard to stage whisper, "Uh oh, here comes that lady with the sock monkeys. Watch her." Kate didn't mind at all. She let folks look on as she propped up the monkeys eating lobster or salt water taffy, or playing in the ocean. Summer vacation never was so entertaining.

The following year, with an extra week's vacation, This youthfully mature woman had some time to herself, so to keep from just cleaning house, eating, sleeping or just doing nothing all the time, she decided to have a little adventure with her sock monkey, Kashie.

Enjoy some relaxing vacation time with Kate and her sock monkeys. You will smile for sure!

Part One

Birth
of a
Sock Monkey

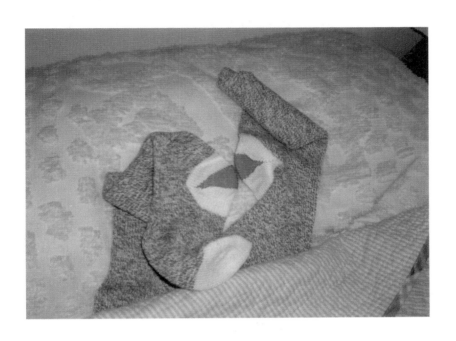

It all begins with the loving embrace of two socks. Heels touch. Their cuffs rolled together

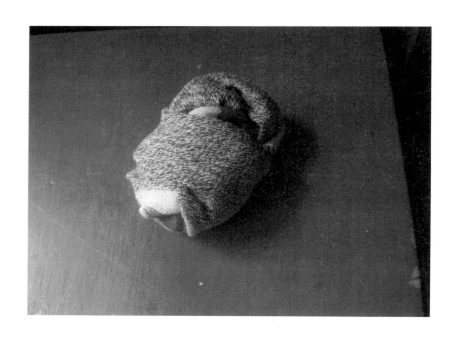

The embryonic sock monkey

begins to grow.

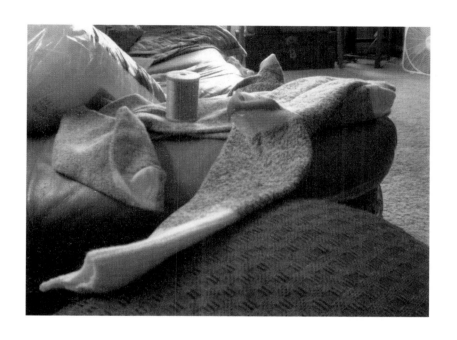

The plans are all laid out.

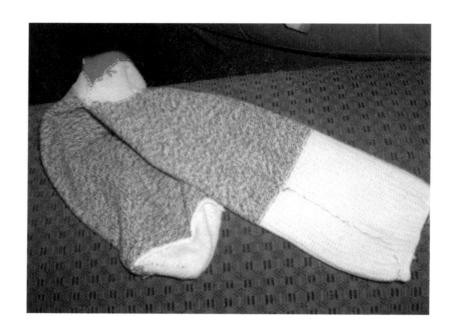

The legs are forming!

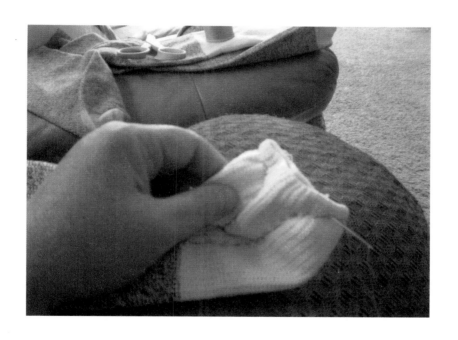

The master creator knows

how it all comes together.

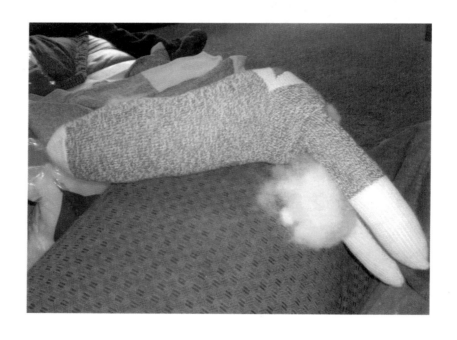

A cloudy shadow prevents us from
knowing if it is a boy or a girl.

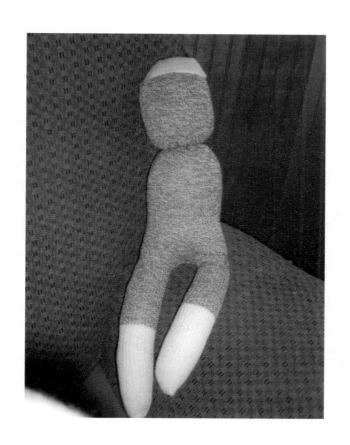

The legs are fully formed!

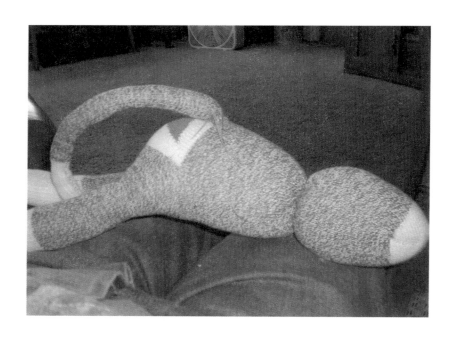

The tail is so long already!

Facial features.. who does this little monkey look like? Mother or Dad?

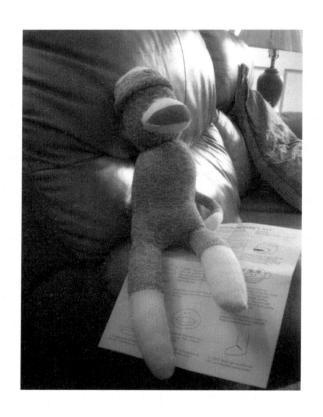

These little legs can sure kick!

Time to add the arms...

Almost finished! Important for character
and vision are the eyes!

Uno Bambino is born! A boy! Look at those ears! I think he looks like his Dad.

Uno Bambino sits with his dad, Henrx. It's the miracle of sock monkey life.

Now you know.

Part Two

Vacation

At

Rockport, MA

Kashie relaxes with her favorite cuppa coffee and a magazine.

This is her other favorite thing to do.

Pay the bills before we leave to go on our vacation trip.

Henrx checks the weather and the news
while Kashie packs the suitcases.

With family ties to Rockport, MA, it is our annual destination of choice for relaxation, good food, and fun.

Here we look at our favorite landmark, Motif #1

First thing we do is walk down to the yacht club, take in the view of the fishing boats and breathe in the salty air.

This is what we see.

Pee-yew! This is what we smell! We examine the lobster traps closely.

We take a walk down Bearskin Neck to peek in the windows of all the shops.

We like the art galleries and the Country Store best of all.

Kashie has a years old tradition of stopping by her most loved spot, the Blue Gate. Every year, she has to touch the gate and peek through the opening.

Flowers bloom everywhere all summer.

Checked in to our room, we enjoy some
shade out on the balcony.

Let's go play on the beach!

Except for our red lips and bums, and Kashie's pom-pom, we are camouflaged in these rocks!

We enjoy some shade in these cool rocks.

Remembering our climbing days when we were young. This driftwood is amazing!

We are looking at tiny hermit crabs and snails in the tide pools. We might get stranded when the tide comes in!

Ahhh, sunbathing on the rocks. Nothing like it in the world.

We enjoy our afternoon snooze.

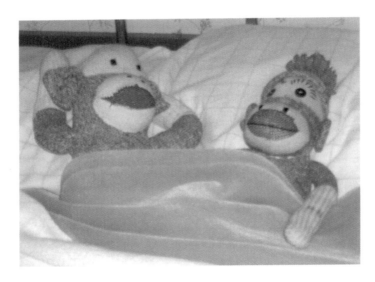

Vacation. Sigh. Ain't it great?!

Hungry now, we grab a bite of Rockport's best pizza. No dieting this week!

Then, some sight-seeing. Our ancestors settled here, so we like to visit the oldest cemeteries and read the headstones.

Every so often, we stop and take in the
ocean. We love sleeping to the sound of
the waves at night.

It's never a trip to Rockport without stopping at Tuck's for some candy. Yum!

Soaking up the sun at the beach again.
Don't let me burn!

Omigawd! Did you see that one over there? These glasses help us to people watch, discreetly.

Early morning, sitting outside. What a
beautiful day this will be!

Donuts! Shh! I told you, no dieting!

4th of July!   We are proud to celebrate!

Lobster in the rough... absolutely delicious!

It's been a delightful vacation!

Kashie's
Week of Time
To Herself

Nothing like it.. early morning sunshine and listening to the world as it awakens.

Checking in with family and friends....

Getting the housework out of the way..

Making the bed. Um, it's probably time to get out the summer sheets... lol!

We'll let Mother Nature dry the dishes
today.   :)

A little polishing and scrubbing and we are all set.. It is nice when everything is done.

A phone call from friend, Susan.

"Lunch tomorrow? Sure! I'd love to!"

"Today, I am spending the afternoon at the lake. See you tomorrow! Bye!"

What's better than some quiet time lakeside?

Relaxing, with my friend, Kate.

Not too many people here... shhh.. Nice!

Red toenails are always a part of summer.
Kate let me paint hers!

Luscious strawberries, warmed by the sun!

I don't swim, but I do love wading in the water. When my tail gets wet, it takes SO long to dry!

Drying my toes in the sun..

Feels so gooood!

mmmm... Stopped for ice cream on the way home. I like peanut butter and Kate likes coffee flavor. The girl who waited on us, thought it funny that we requested two spoons!

Kate and I sharing ice cream and
sunshine together!

Out to lunch at Kimballs with best friends,
Susan and Steven...

When we get together, Steven, Susan, Kate
and Kashie have belly full of laughs!

This meal looks healthy. Not to worry...
We'll have an ice cream sundae for
dessert!

This day of quiet vacation, Kashie is taking
a mindful walk.

Daisies! Our mostest favorite flower!

This li'l critter likes the taste!

See the damaged daisy? You don't have to perfect to be part of a great bunch. Can you find the spider?

Wild strawberries...

Close up view of these tiny purple flowers.

Sitting in a tree... always comfy for Kashie

Other things to see on our quiet walk, like
this very respectful peaceable rock.

And poppies! Whenever we say poppies,
we always sound like the witch in the
Wizard of Oz.. Poppies!

Arranging some of the flowers we picked today. Spider not included.

He loves me... he loves me not...well, let's
find out....

Contemplating the finish... I hope it comes
out the way she wants it to...

Uh oh, someone's been watching....

It seems that Purdy Mae Butterbean is envious of all the attention that Kashie, the sock monkey has been getting. It appears Purdy is planning something!

Ohhh... Purdy can't stand waiting for the finish to plucking daisy petals. She has to find out for herself, and quickly!

Purdy is going to find the answer and find it out soon. He loves me, he loves me not, ohhh... he loves me!

And now, some contemplative creative
time, drawing...

A little rough, but coming out nicely...

Drawing is so calming...

For now, Kashie is content to sit on the old bookshelf, in front of the dusty air conditioner with her friends, until the next adventure with Kate.

She'll read to Henrx and Uno Bambino,
some of Kate's tales, and enjoy her own
sock monkey life....

THE END

about the authors...

I'm **Kate Taylor**.

I hail from a small town in New Hampshire. I am a nationally certified Activities Director and enjoy writing, playing the piano and watercolor painting. I am also the author of The Pink Eraser, and co-author with Jeffrey Underwood of Treason's Truth; Mac Alpin's Scotland, and Eagle's Eclipse; America Before Columbus. We have just recently published Rule of Thumb & Fingers. Jeff and I are also currently working on yet another tale of historical fiction. I used to live vicariously through my sock monkeys much of the time. Now, life lived primarily by me with my brown friends at my side is exciting and rewarding, bringing me joy every day. And the unique blend that I share with Jeff Underwood, matches none. I find Jeff's enthusiasm, turquoise aura, and humor to be a catalyst to my writing.

Jeffrey Underwood here.

I was once a practicing registered nurse. After so many years of that in Seattle, I finally followed my heart...nurturing by the pen instead of by the stethoscope. And along this journey, I met the very special Kate Taylor. We live 3000 miles away from one another. Kate and I have written a number of books together...principally by texting. Kate's fresh perspective, quick wit, and her ability to find a ray of pink light in any situation, inspire me.

So, read us and learn the lessons of our experience and you might find miracles occurring in your life as well.

15793452R10050

Made in the USA
Charleston, SC
21 November 2012